01

You've given some shape to your business idea and defined the foundations for developing it. In this part of 'Launch Your Own Creative Successful Business', you'll explore the different aspects that will allow your business to work.

You'll look at three main areas...

Customers
To determine who is buying your product, and why

Your business process
The different elements that make up your business

Relationships
The different associations you have to recognise and develop to ensure your product or service reaches your customers.

www.nesta.org.uk

02

WHO'S BUYING?

Before you spend any more time developing the business, you should check that your activity meets a genuine need. If it doesn't, then there may not be much point going any further.

At this point it will be useful to revisit the business idea questions highlighted earlier:

- What is it that I do?
- Why should my customers care?
- Is there a need for what I'm offering?
- Will there be sufficient demand?
- Will that generate sufficient reward for me to move forward?

Basing your answers on purely a gut feeling might be a little flimsy to risk your business future on, so you need to gather some real evidence. This gathering of evidence is called market research. The two main things to consider at this stage are: who is your customer; and how does your product or service benefit them?

01 Defining Your Customer

First, identify who would like to buy your product or service. It's more important to work out who your customers are before you work out how you're going to behave with them. Customers come in many shapes and sizes, and you need to be able to respond to all of them. Make a list of as many types of customers as you can and estimate how many would want your product or service.

02 Outlining the Benefit to Customers

Then, make explicit what benefit your product or service will bring to each of the customer types. For example:

> *I have identified that need W is not being met by anybody (or certainly not well enough). I propose offering X as a solution to this need. Y will be the benefit to my customer /client and for this I will expect to charge Z.*

If you can't afford to use a market research company, you can carry this out yourself. For example:

Desk Research: Use the internet to find out about competitors' products or services and keep up to date with their activities, news stories, client days and case studies. This will give you an idea of what customers are buying, how much they'll pay and how your product or service offers something new or different.

Published Market Research: Some information on general trends can be accessed for free. You can also buy reports on market trends from a variety of commercial companies. This can help confirm the need or demand for your product or service, and allow you to clearly target your customers.

Field Research: This includes both qualitative and quantitative research. Qualitative research can identify individuals' feelings and attitudes to a product or service, and lead to suggested improvements. Quantitative research provides statistical information, for example, how many potential customers there are, their socio-economic background, age profile, and purchasing habits.

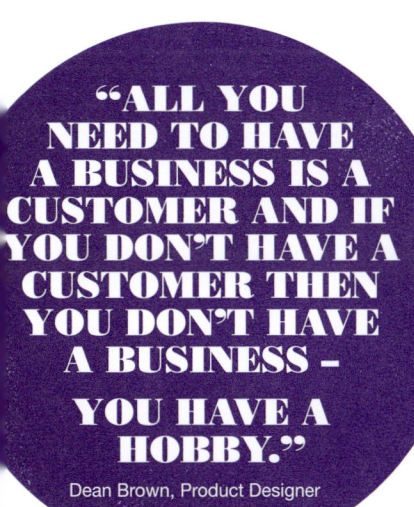

> "ALL YOU NEED TO HAVE A BUSINESS IS A CUSTOMER AND IF YOU DON'T HAVE A CUSTOMER THEN YOU DON'T HAVE A BUSINESS – YOU HAVE A HOBBY."
>
> Dean Brown, Product Designer

04

WHO'S BUYING?

For qualitative research, you can put together a formal focus group, or just do something more informal – as was the case with Innocent Smoothies.

> **Innocent Smoothies**
>
> Three graduates tested their fruit smoothie drinks at a music festival in London. People were invited to put the empty cartons in bins marked YES and NO depending on whether they liked the product. At the end of the festival the YES bins were full. After getting investment they launched the product and the rest is history.

Use the earlier Evidence Modelling exercise to help you identify the needs and benefits associated with your product or service. In Worksheet 03a: Your Customers is a table that you can complete for each customer group. This will help you record and establish viable income streams for each customer group.

Worksheet 03a: Your customers

03a Your Customers

Do

Use this worksheet to build a picture of your potential customers and customer groups. You might want to copy the worksheet and try it several times for different customer groups.

Write onto the stickies and place them onto the worksheet. If you want to change it later simply remove the sticky and try again.

You can do this informally, from memory, or with friends or colleagues. Ideally, you should be talking to your potential customers who will buy your product or service and, if different, the end users.

Be open to feedback and fresh perspectives as people can come up with suggestions you haven't considered.

What do you call this customer group?					
Draw them – or stick a 'found' picture here		What are their needs?			
		What are you offering them?			
How many are there?	How many of those will you reach?	How frequently?	How much will they pay?	Potential total income?	

Nesta...

Choosing your path — What you need to make your business work

You can start to complete the table by talking to your friends and family, but ideally you should also be talking to your potential customers, and anyone who could be involved in supplying your products or services to them.

Be open to feedback and fresh perspectives, as people can come up with suggestions you haven't considered. Your local business support agency, libraries and online resources like the British Library Business and IP Centre all host information that can support your research.

The specific questions you ask during your research will depend upon the nature of your business. However, the key information you need is:

- How big is your potential market?
- Roughly and realistically how many people can you get your idea in front of?
- How are you going to engage with them?
- How many of them will buy it?
- Is this a big enough group to meet your income needs?

If demand is big enough to meet your needs then you can proceed. If not, then maybe it's time to think again. You could improve your idea, or look into reaching more people by broadening the scope of your offer.

Market research can be a very challenging process. You're opening up your idea to feedback and criticism – and the possibility there isn't enough demand or paying customers to make it a viable business.

However, don't be tempted to avoid it. If your analysis of the market potential is flawed at this stage, you'll probably come out with a flawed business design.

06

WHO'S BUYING?

Try to stay objective. Remember the aim is to test whether your idea has application as a good business idea. At this stage it's easy to reframe the idea, develop it or drop it and start again. This becomes more difficult as time goes on, and you've invested money and energy in the idea.

CREATING A SUSTAINABLE BUSINESS

There are three key aspects to creating a sustainable business:

01 Having a clear idea of what you want your business to do.

02 Knowing that there'll be an audience or market for what you're going to offer.

03 Developing a business process that allows you to offer this to customers and sell it for more than it costs to produce.

> "Starting a business can be a daunting but nonetheless exciting prospect. Being given the tools to help you break down exactly what you need to do and when you need to do it has helped me manage my business needs one step at a time instead of visualising a mammoth task and not knowing where to start."

Rachel Horrocks, Product Designer.

07

So far you've used Evidence Modelling to help you explore point 01 and Who's Buying to explore point 02. The next sections help you explore point 03.

One way to understand how a business works is to think of your business activity in terms of promises:

- You promise your customers that you'll deliver either a product or a service
- Your customers will have an expectation that this promise is going to be kept, and
- You work with others to enable that promise to be delivered.

These make a 'promise triangle' between you, your customer and the qualities of your product or service.

The Promise Triangle

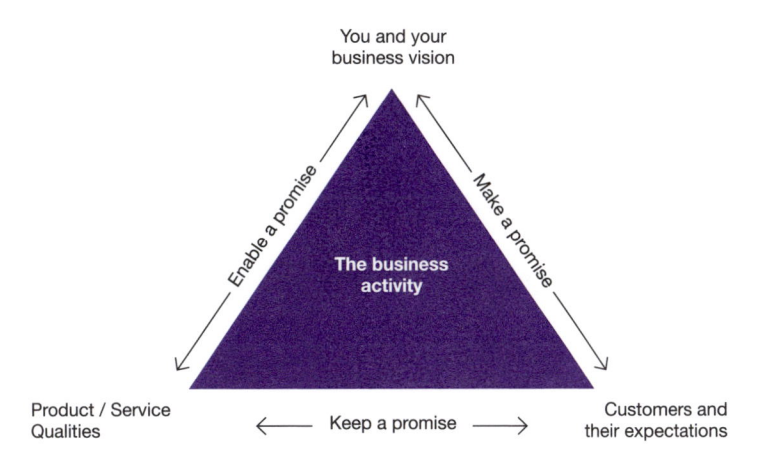

```
                    You and your
                    business vision
                         /\
                        /  \
              Enable   /    \   Make
              a promise/      \  a promise
                     /  The    \
                    / business  \
                   /  activity   \
                  /_____\
   Product / Service  ← Keep a promise →  Customers and
   Qualities                              their expectations
```

Any business involves a number of different areas, and it's unlikely you're going to undertake them all yourself. Therefore, you'll need to involve others and build relationships to help you deliver on the promises.

www.nesta.org.uk

08

CREATING A SUSTAINABLE BUSINESS

Most innovative individuals rely on their creativity and inventiveness to drive their businesses, controlling every aspect of activity themselves. Because this energy and control can be difficult to sustain, this approach can cause issues for you and your business's wellbeing. Besides, you probably also only have interest, skills, and expertise in certain areas of your business. Frequently, it will be too expensive and time-consuming for you to acquire expertise in all areas.

You need to establish the roles your business needs, and which of them you'll undertake. To do this you need to:

- Identify where your personal skills and interests fit within your business;
- Understand what you need to add to your own skills in order to create a complete set of business skills; and
- Identify the relationships you need to build with other people and businesses to make your business succeed.

Techniques we call Blueprint Modelling and Relationship Modelling will help with this. Blueprint Modelling helps you describe the process of your business, while Relationship Modelling identifies four areas of activity in which you can develop a role or relationships to support your business.

If you can build a business model that allows your business to live beyond your direct involvement, it will mean that your ideas will have been transferred and embedded in others. It will also mean that you can extract financial, creative or social value from your business whilst you go off to work on other ideas.

Before we explore Relationship Modelling further, you need to work out the various aspects of your business and how they fit together: the process of your business. To do this, we use Blueprint Modelling.

09

BLUEPRINT MODELLING

A blueprint is a detailed plan or design that explains how something is expected to work. So this exercise will help you visualise how your business will actually function, and describe how business will be done. It will help you identify all the activities involved in a yearly overview down to a day-to-day plan.

> "Blueprint Modelling is a fantastically useful (life-changing!) tool that we are using to break down the goals we want to achieve. Such a simple thing, but so incredibly helpful if you are a creative perfectionist!"
>
> Zoe Sinclair, Artist.

Before you start developing your business blueprint, let's look at some operational factors you'll need to consider.

There are lots of different types of businesses specialising in different sorts of activities. For example, how a jeweller operates is very different from a film or TV production company. However, even in this example there are similarities. All businesses, whether product or service based, have a process. This process consists of a client engagement phase, a development phase and a delivery phase.

Engagement Stage: This is the time that it takes to plan who your prospective clients are and to persuade them to buy products or services from you.

Development Stage: This is the time that it takes to develop your product or service for your customers.

Delivery Stage: This is the time it takes to get your product or service to your customer.

10

BLUEPRINT MODELLING

All of these activities take place either in front of the customer, which we call 'Onstage', or out of sight of the customer, which we call 'Backstage'. The examples in the diagram below show how this process might look for a design company.

Areas shaded in grey are things that can't be directly charged to the customer: you can't bill your client for market research, promotion or the cost of selling to customers. You need to fund these from your profit margin. This is why businesses that can't get beyond the engagement stage, or that are purely focused on backroom research and development, will ultimately fail.

Use Part A: Operational Stages of Worksheet 03b: Blueprint Modelling and place the stickies to show which parts of your business take place Backstage and Onstage, and at what parts of the delivery process from engagement to delivery.

03b Blueprint Modelling

Do

This exercise will help you visualise how your business will function and describe how business will be done.

PART A: Operational Stages. Every business has these:

01 Engagement Stage: The time that it takes to plan who your prospective customers are and how to persuade them to buy from you.

02 Development Stage: The time that it takes to design and create your offer.

03 Delivery stage: The time it takes to get your product or service to your customer.

Activities take place either in front of the customer – 'Onstage' – or out of sight of the customer – 'Backstage'.

Write stickies for your business activities and place them in the relevant box. Consider doing this in a small group or as a pair.

Areas shaded in grey represent activities that are costs that cannot be charged to a customer.

PART B: Blueprint Modelling. Map out all the steps you will need to take to deliver your product or service, in a linear flow diagram. Map the entire process in very small steps. Use a sticky for each step.

Nesta...

	Part A		Part B
	Backstage	Onstage	Starting here
Engagement	e.g. things like customer and market research	e.g. things like networking or exhibiting at trade-shows	↓
			↓
Development	e.g. things like developing briefs and ideas	e.g. things like showing customers early prototypes	↓
			↓
Delivery	e.g. things like design reviews and making decisions	e.g. things like presenting to a customer or client	↓
			↓
			Finishing here

11

Drawing a Blueprint[1]

A simple way of understanding how your business will deliver its products and services is to draw, using flow diagrams, the various stages of generating, realising and distributing a product or service. You can create a blueprint by mapping out how you're going to come up with the idea, how you're going to have the idea realised and how you're going to deliver it to your customer.

A good starting point is to answer the following questions:

- **How do I imagine my business operating?**
- **How will I find and engage my customers?**
- **How will I generate what they want?**
- **How will I distribute what I generate?**

You might find it easiest to imagine yourself at the point of delivering the product or service to the client and work backwards.

Each drawing or business blueprint will look different. Over the page are two examples, one showing a simplified process for a furniture design company and the other a more detailed example mapping a trip to the airport and boarding a plane in which you will see the detailed tasks that need to be undertaken and the different people involved in this.

---

[1] Blueprint modelling has been developed with reference to the work of Bill and Gillian Hollins in their book 'Over the Horizon', published by Wiley.

12

BLUEPRINT MODELLING

Diagram 01
Simplified business blueprint for a product-based furniture company.

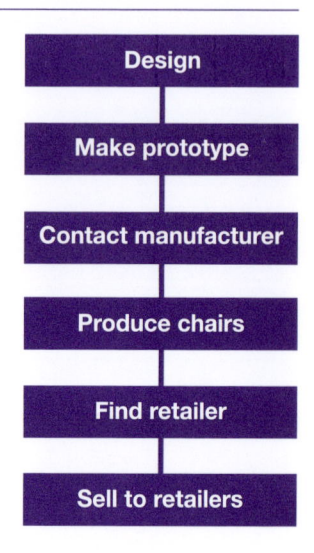

- Design
- Make prototype
- Contact manufacturer
- Produce chairs
- Find retailer
- Sell to retailers

The objectives of these flow diagrams are to identify:

- The tasks that need to be undertaken at each stage of your business, and
- The different people involved in delivering these activities.

From this process you can see where the critical stages are, where bottlenecks may occur and where the process might break down because you don't have the necessary expertise or resources. This will allow you to see how much of the business you need to develop and manage.

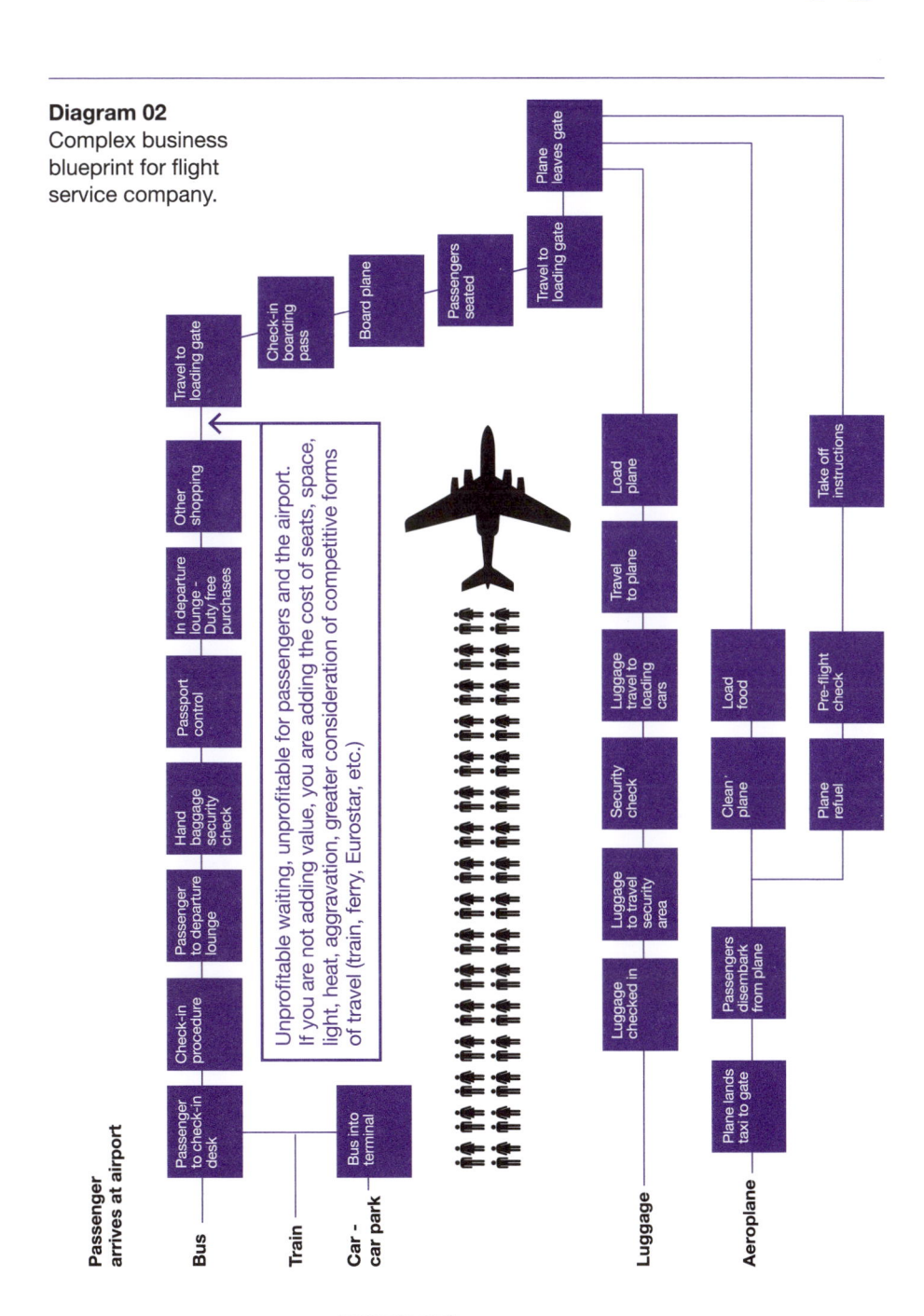

Diagram 02
Complex business blueprint for flight service company.

Unprofitable waiting, unprofitable for passengers and the airport. If you are not adding value, you are adding the cost of seats, space, light, heat, aggravation, greater consideration of competitive forms of travel (train, ferry, Eurostar, etc.).

Passenger arrives at airport

- **Bus**: Passenger to check-in desk → Check-in procedure → Passenger to departure lounge → Hand baggage security check → Passport control → In departure lounge - Duty free purchases → Other shopping → Travel to loading gate → Check-in boarding pass → Board plane → Passengers seated → Travel to loading gate → Plane leaves gate
- **Train**
- **Car - car park**: Bus into terminal

Luggage: Luggage checked in → Luggage to travel security area → Security check → Luggage travel to loading cars → Travel to plane → Load plane

Aeroplane: Plane lands taxi to gate → Passengers disembark from plane → Clean plane → Load food → Plane refuel → Pre-flight check → Take off instructions

www.nesta.org.uk

14

BLUEPRINT
MODELLING

Developing Your Business Blueprint

There are three rules to blueprinting:

- Do it in small steps
- Map the entire process
- Include as much detail as possible.

Using Part B of Worksheet 03b: Blueprint Modelling, create a flow diagram of your business idea. Remember to identify and detail all the stages that need to take place to realise your idea.

In your business there may be many processes that happen simultaneously, so you may need several blueprints to create the whole picture.

Blueprint Model Example 1

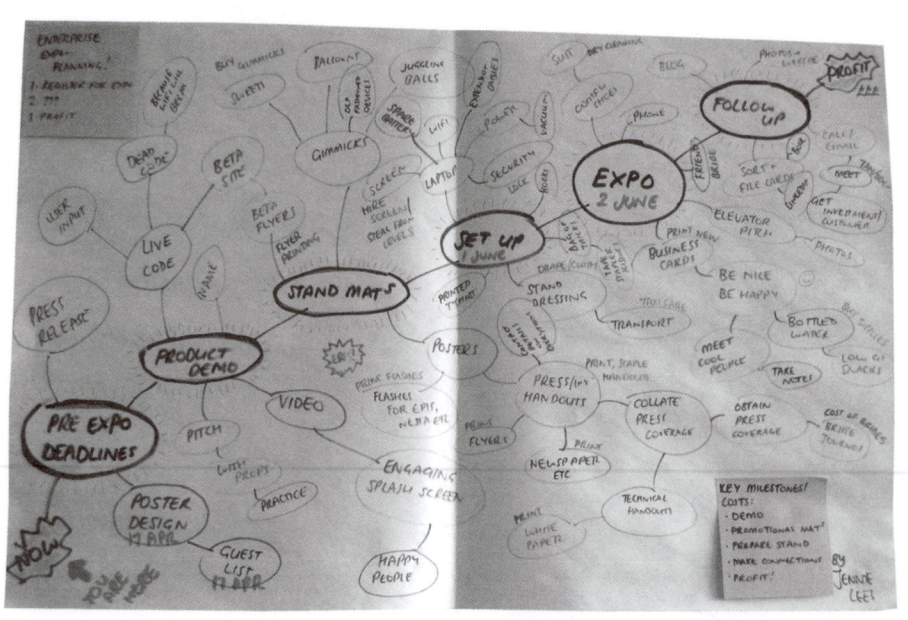

15

Refer to Part A: Operational Stages of Worksheet 03b to identify which parts of your business are happening in front of the customer and those that are behind the scenes. You can then draw separate blueprints for onstage and backstage activity, and also overlay this information with your existing blueprint. This should give you a clear insight into exactly how your business might operate.

On these pages are some examples of blueprints. You'll see that the number of stages and styles used vary – proof that there's no right or wrong way to develop your blueprint.

Blueprint Model Example 2

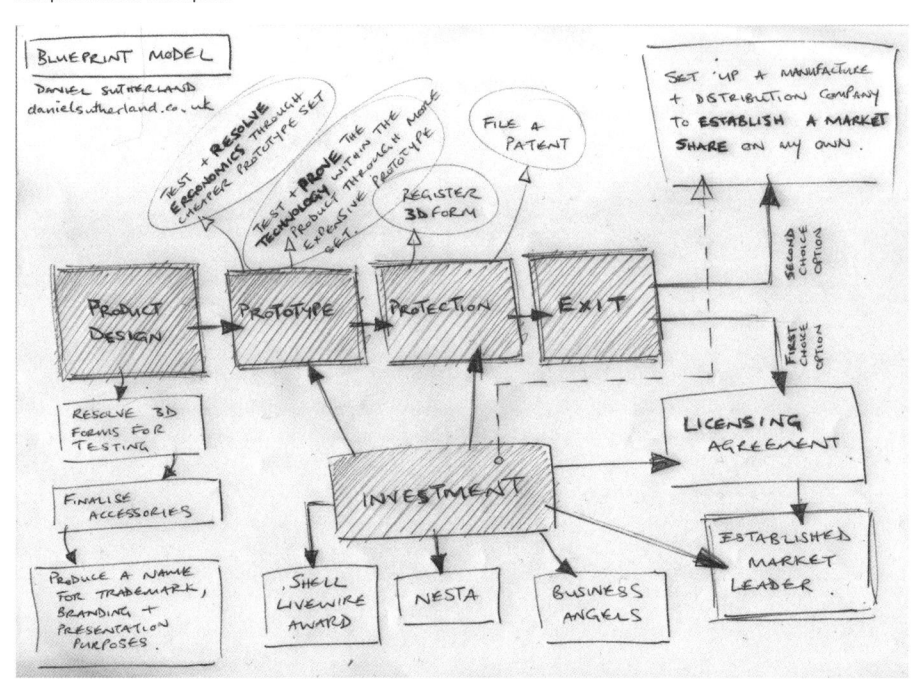

www.nesta.org.uk

16

RELATIONSHIP MODELLING

Blueprinting is one part of understanding how your business works and where you might need assistance from others. In this section you'll focus on the relationships you need to make for your business process to work. Think about the following:

- **How do you find people to help you?**
- **Why would anybody want to help you?**
- **What sort of deal can you expect?**

The first step in Relationship Modelling is to understand the four areas of activity that are necessary to support your business: the Generator, Realiser, Distributor and Customer:

Generator/Idea Generator: key activities are originating, forming and synthesising ideas; direction, design and concept development. This role describes the process of forming and synthesising ideas. It's important in creativity, and concept development. If this is the area where you're most familiar and where you think all your strengths lie, it's probably where you're tempted to spend all your time.

Realiser: key activities include transforming ideas into finished product, services and experiences; manufacture and content production. This role describes the process of transforming raw materials or ideas, such as a film script or a piece of sheet music, as well as physical materials, into a finished product.

Distributor: key activities encompass distributing finished products, services and experiences; delivery, sales and marketing. This role describes the purchase of finished products or services for resale, or the co-ordination and distribution of finished products or services.

Customer: key activities include buying, consuming, utilising or experiencing the product or service. This role receives, buys or consumes an item or service.

All four areas need to be in place for your business to survive. However, your business does not need to do all these things itself, and can achieve them through building relationships with others.

The areas can be overlaid with the activities defined on your blueprint. The diagram below shows the four activity areas overlaid with the blueprint activities of the furniture company we looked at previously on page 12.

Diagram 03: Areas of Business Activity

Generator	**Realiser**
Design	Make prototype
	Contact manufacturer
	Produce chairs
Customer	**Distributor**
	Find retailer
	Sell to retailers

You can see that there are only three of the four activity areas linked together in the relationship for the furniture design company. They don't sell directly to customers and instead work with distributors and intermediaries – therefore there are no activities shown in the 'customer' section.

www.nesta.org.uk

18

RELATIONSHIP MODELLING

There's nothing uncommon about this type of relationship, but the implications for the business are significant. The distributors will charge for their service, either as a commission or as a mark-up on price, such as from wholesale to retail. Some distributors cover whole countries (as in the film industry), while others are more targeted (as with fashion retailers). The nature of your product and how it's distributed will determine whether you have to make one relationship or develop many.

The type of business you're creating and the way you want to run it will determine which activity areas are involved.

Defining Your Relationships

Using Part B of Workbook 03c: Relationship Modelling, highlight activities from your Blueprint Model that correspond to any of the four key areas (generator, realiser, distributor and customer).

Identify where your skills and interests lie.
Ask yourself:

- Who will you need to build relationships with in order to cover the other areas?

- Who is giving or receiving the money in each of these relationships?

- What will be the implications of your relationship sequence on how much you need to charge and when you get paid?

- Is this something you'll be able to manage? If not, what additional resources will you need?

Spend time exploring different scenarios to understand the most effective ones for your idea. You're prototyping your business, so it's worth considering many different designs of your business model at this stage.

Building Relationships

All businesses depend on others for their survival. You're always buying products and services from others, or supplying products and services to others.

For a successful combination, each relationship needs to be based on mutual trust and support. If some relationships collapse, they can have a significant effect on the activity of the business. So it's important to have a good understanding of who's supporting who in each relationship, and who's supporting your 'Promise Triangle'.

When you're in the buying role, you need to be clear about what you want, when you want it, the quality and consistency, how much it will cost, and when and how you're going to pay.

If you're looking to buy a computer from Dell, for example, you can have a high expectation that it will arrive as expected, and you'll know what you'll be charged and when it will be delivered. This is because Dell has clearly defined what it can and cannot do. This is the minimum that you should expect from any relationship.

Why Would Anybody Want to Help You With Your Business?

It's critical that any relationship you pursue and develop creates a win-win situation for both parties.

What differentiates your relationships with a supplier or distributor and other people's relationships with the same supplier is the experience. A good experience will prolong and strengthen the relationship; a bad experience will bring the relationship into question.

20

RELATIONSHIP MODELLING

Historically, business relationships were mainly about transactions. The manufacturer didn't necessarily consider the customers' needs or wants to any great degree. This is no longer the case, and every business has a large number of potential partners to choose from to build relationships with.

In order to build good relationships there are some points you should bear in mind:

- You need to be informed about your customers' or partners' needs and understand how they will benefit from the relationship.

- A relationship has not been established just because you think it has. Both parties need to be involved.

- Relationships are based upon attitudes. Initially you'll rely on trust and honesty and then you can develop ties, all of which need to be earned and sustained.

- Relationships create a mutual way of thinking and the depth of this will increase with the longevity, frequency and quality of your transactions.

When building a relationship the customer should be seen as a resource with whom the firm can create a valued solution based on a level of co-operation. In terms of partners, suppliers and other intermediaries, firms will not work with each other from a win-lose perspective but they will from a win-win one, where both parties are better off as partners.

Think about your own situation and write down answers to the following questions.

- What's appealing about your business for the:

    Generator?

    Realiser?

    Distributor?

    Customer?

- What can you currently offer them?
- Is that enough, and if not, what do you need to offer for them to want to work with you?
- What are you going to have to do to make that happen?
- What additional resources, skills, people and information might you need to get there?
- What impact will that have on your finances and planning?

It's vital to be able to show when you will be paid and how you will collect the funds. Many apparently successful businesses fail in their first few years because they owe their suppliers money, which they can't pay because they haven't been paid themselves by their clients. It is therefore vital to identify all the people involved in the flow of money around your business.

What Sort of Deal Can You Expect?

On initiating a relationship and starting a conversation with potential partners and suppliers, you must know and be able to articulate:

- What you want out of the relationship;
- What you are going to offer to your partner; and
- Why it will benefit them.

22

CONTRACTS AND AGREEMENTS

Contracts and agreements help ensure that business transactions are clearly understood by and acceptable to the parties concerned. It should include a clear written specification of what you are going to do, the costs to the client and your payment terms. The latter is important to ensure that you get paid the right amount and on time.

Specification

This should include:

- A description of the project based on the client brief

- How much time it will take you to deliver

- When you will provide progress reports or staged viewings of work-in-progress

- The number of changes the client can make without charge

- Size, shape, colour, text, font and any other specific details that are vital to the specification

- What penalties you will incur if you do not deliver to schedule

- Details of the price for all the elements of the project, including management fees, print costs, VAT etc.

- Your payment terms stating how and at what stages of the project you want to get paid.

Payment Terms

Clearly stating your payment terms is important as many small businesses fail due to poor cash flow management. You need to know when you need to be paid and how much that should be.

If the job will take a while then set a series of staged payments, for example, 40% on the project being commissioned, 30% mid-stage, and 30% on completion.

If you have to purchase expensive materials then ask the client to pay for this in advance then follow up with a staged payment or remainder on completion.

You might prefer to present a delivery note and request cash or a cheque on completion rather than submitting an invoice. When you submit an invoice then clearly state the payment terms, for example, seven days or 30 days. Keep records of the invoices you have sent out, when they were paid and when they are overdue. Use your discretion as to when to send a reminder for outstanding payments but don't avoid it. Remember – if you've done the work, you're owed the money!

Contract/Agreement Sign Off

Send two copies of contract/agreement to the client for them to sign off. Make it clear that work will not start until you receive a signed copy. This becomes a legally binding agreement with clear terms and conditions for both parties.

A solicitor can draw up a standard contract covering these areas that you can modify for each client. Alternatively trade associations may have sample contracts that you can use. Remember, you are doing this to protect yourself and your customers from misunderstandings, disagreements and crossed wires.

Sale or Return

This is where you negotiate a selling figure with a gallery or outlet, of which they take a percentage with you receiving the balance when the item is sold. In this case you have to pay for all materials up front.

It is common for galleries and outlets to use sale or return to see if your work will sell before committing to buying up front. You should consider limiting the number of items you will leave on a sale or return basis.

24

BEFORE WE MOVE ON

The activities and guides in this handbook have helped you identify your customers, explore the connecting aspects of your business, and the various relationships you will want to develop to help your business move forward.

To summarise:

- You have identified your customer base and checked there's a need for your product or service at the price you want to charge.

- You understand the interrelation of your business vision, your customer expectations, and the qualities of your product or service.

- Blueprint Modelling helped you turn your draft operational plan into a more detailed picture.

- Relationship Modelling introduced different types of relationships you need to develop in the four key areas of business activity: Generator, Realiser, Distributor and Customer.

- You considered contractual details for the payment terms that suit your needs.

With what you've found out about roles and responsibilities, go back and update your blueprint. Add how you'll build and manage the relationships within your relationship model (for example, researching suppliers and meeting distributors) and the flow of money around those relationships (for example, paying suppliers and invoicing customers).

In handbook 04: **In it for the long haul** we look at:

- Different ways of communicating with customers through the marketing mix.

- Developing a marketing plan

- Controlling your business finances to ensure you have a sustainable business that meets your aspirations.